The Mysterious Affair at Styles (Illustrated)

—

Agatha Christie

—

Adapted for kids aged 9-12, Key Stage 2 - Key Stage-3, Grade 4 - Grade 7 by Lazlo Ferran

Classics adapted by Lazlo Ferran:

The Mysterious Affair at Styles – Adapted For Kids
The Mysterious Affair at Styles – Adapted For Kids – Large Print
The Mysterious Affair at Styles – Kids Colouring Book
The Mysterious Affair at Styles – Kids Fun Exercise Book
The Mysterious Affair at Styles – For EFL/ESL Level B2 Students
The Mysterious Affair at Styles – Vocabulary Stretcher
The Secret Adversary – Adapted For Kids (US and UK Editions)
The Secret Adversary – For Kids (US and UK Editions) – Large Print
The Secret Adversary – Kids Colouring Book
The Secret Adversary – Kids Fun Exercise Book
The Secret Adversary – For EFL/ESL Level B2 Students (US and UK Editions)
The Secret Adversary – Vocabulary Stretcher (US and UK Editions)
Frankenstein – Adapted For Kids
Frankenstein – Adapted For Kids – Large Print
Frankenstein – Kids Colouring Book
Frankenstein – Kids Fun Exercise Book
Frankenstein – For EFL/ESL Level B2 Students
Frankenstein – Vocabulary Stretcher
MacBeth – Adapted For Kids
MacBeth – Kids Colouring Book
MacBeth – Kids Fun Exercise Book
MacBeth – Adapted For Kids – Large Print
MacBeth – For EFL/ESL Level B2 Students
MacBeth – Vocabulary Stretcher

Other books by Lazlo Ferran:

Ordo Lupus and the Temple Gate
Too Bright the Sun
The Hole Inside the Earth

Hercule Poirot

Styles Court

Contents

Chapter 1—I go to Styles

Detective Poirot was an amazing looking, little man. He wasn't more than five feet, four inches tall, but walked with great dignity. His head was exactly the shape of an egg, and he always held it a little on one side. His moustache was very stiff and military, and his clothes were always neat. I believe a speck of dust would have caused him more pain than a bullet wound.

"We will arrange the facts," Poirot would say. "Those of no importance, pouf!"—he screwed up his baby face and puffed out his cheeks in a funny way—"blow them away!"

"That's good," I replied, "but how are you going to decide what is important and what isn't?"

"One fact leads to another. This fact fits with that. Another fact doesn't fit. We examine. We search. And that little curious fact, that little detail that will not fit, we put it here! No detail is too small."

As a Belgian detective, he had solved some of the most difficult cases of the day. When he spoke I listened, because I wanted to be a detective too!

So how did I come to work with Poirot on one of the most famous murder cases in England?

I was a soldier and had been wounded in the First World War. After spending a few months recovering in a gloomy hospital, I bumped into my childhood friend, John Cavendish. We had a good chat, and he invited me to spend my rest at his home, Styles Court.

"Mother will be happy to see you again—after all those years," he added.

"Your mother keeps well?" I asked.

"Oh, yes. I suppose you know that she married again after dad died? Now she is Mrs Emily Inglethorp."

I was surprised. John's mother would be seventy by now. I remembered her as a rich and generous woman.

Lawrence, John's younger brother, had often been sick as a child. He qualified as a doctor but gave it up to become writer, without success. John had become a lawyer but gave it up to live in luxury at the family's big house in the country. He married two years before and took his wife to live with him at Styles.

John noticed my surprise at the news of his mother's remarriage and added:

"Her husband is a nasty man too! He's Eve's .... Do you remember Eve?"

"No."

"Well, she is mother's assistant now!"

"You were going to say—?"

"Yes. My new stepfather is a cousin of Eve's. He's got a big, black beard and wears shiny leather boots all the time! Nobody likes him, except mum. I think he just wants her money!"

It was a still, warm day in early July when I arrived at Styles. As we turned in at the lodge gates, John said:

"I wonder if we've time to pick up Cynthia. No, she'll have started from the hospital by now."

"Your wife?"

"No, Cynthia is an orphan and poor. My mother came to the rescue, and Cynthia has been with us nearly two years now. She works in the Hospital at Tadminster, seven miles away."

As he spoke the last words, we stopped in front of the fine old house. A lady in a checked skirt, who was bending over a flower bed, stood up at our approach.

"Hello Eve, here's our wounded hero! Mr. Hastings. John this is Miss. Eve Howard."

Eve shook hands with a strong, grip. She had very blue eyes in a sunburnt face. She was a pleasant-looking woman of about forty, with a deep voice and had a large, sensible, square body, with feet in good, thick boots to match. She spoke in short phrases.

"Weeds grow like house fires. Better be careful."

"Where's tea to-day—inside or out?" John asked Eve.

"Out."

Eve led the way round the house to where tea was spread under the shade of a large sycamore.

A figure rose from one of the cane chairs.

"My wife," said John.

I shall never forget my first sight of Mary Cavendish. She had beautiful, brown eyes that seemed to show a deep calmness. I shall never forget them. She said hello in a clear voice, and we sat down to drink some tea.

A familiar voice floated came from the open glass door nearby. The door swung open and a white-haired, old lady stepped out of it onto the lawn. A man with a big, black beard followed her. The old lady recognised me and said:

"Hello Mr Hastings. This is Alfred, my husband."

I looked with curiosity at Alfred. His beard was one of the longest and blackest I have ever seen. He wore gold-rimmed glasses, and reminded me of an actor, because his face hid all emotions. His voice was deep but sounded bored:

"This is a pleasure, Mr. Hastings," he said. Then, turning to the old lady: "Emily dearest, I think that cushion is a bit damp. Have you always been a soldier Mr. Hastings?"

"No, before the war I worked for a bank."

A young girl in volunteer nursing uniform ran lightly across the lawn.

"Why, Cynthia, you are late to-day. This is Mr. Hastings— Miss Murdoch. She works in a hospital pharmacy, providing medicine."

Cynthia Murdoch was young and full of life. She had red hair and small, white hands. She sat on the grass and asked me to sit beside her.

I sat down and asked her:

"You work at Tadminster, don't you, Miss Murdoch?"

She nodded.

"How many people do you poison?" I asked, smiling.

Cynthia smiled too.

"Oh, hundreds!" she said, laughing.

My hostess turned to me and said.

"John will show you your room. Supper is at half-past seven. We are at war, so nothing is wasted here—every scrap of waste paper is saved and sent away in sacks."

John took me up the broad staircase, which forked right and left half-way to different wings of the building. My room was in the left wing.

John left me, and a few minutes later I was looking out of the window when a very dark man stepped out from the shadow of a tree and walked across the lawn. It was John's younger brother, Lawrence Cavendish. He looked angry, and I wondered why.

The evening passed pleasantly enough and I dreamed that night of that interesting woman, Mary Cavendish.

The next morning dawned bright and sunny. Mary took me for a charming afternoon walk in the woods. We returned about five. As we entered the large hall, John called us both into the lounge. He looked upset and told us:

"Look here, Mary, Eve's had a row with Alfred Inglethorp, and she's leaving."

"Eve? Leaving?"

John nodded sadly.

"Yes; you see she went to mother, and—Oh,—here's Eve herself."

Eve Howard entered. Her lips were set grimly together, and she carried a small suitcase. She looked excited, determined and slightly defensive.

She burst out, "I've spoken my mind!"

"My dear Eve," cried Mary Cavendish, "this can't be true!"

Miss Howard nodded grimly.

"True enough! I told Mrs. Inglethorp, 'Emily, you're an old fool. Alfred's twenty years younger than you. He married you for money! Well, don't let him have too much of it. Farmer Raikes has got a very pretty young wife. Just ask Alfred how much time he spends over there.' Mrs. Inglethorp was very angry. I told her, 'That man will murder you in your bed one day. He's bad!'"

"What did she say?"

"She said the sooner I left her house the better, so I'm going."

"But not now?"

"This minute!"

We were shocked, but we couldn't change her mind. John went to look up the trains times. His wife, Mary, followed him, saying she would try to persuade Mrs. Inglethorp to apologize.

As she left the room, Miss Howard's face changed. She leant towards me.

"Mr. Hastings, can I trust you?"

I was a little startled. She laid her hand on my arm and sank her voice to a whisper.

"Look after Emily Inglethorp. They're all trying to get money out of her. Above all, Mr. Hastings, watch that devil—her husband!"

As the Rolls Royce drove away, Mary Cavendish suddenly walked across the lawn to meet a tall, bearded man who had been walking toward the house. Her cheeks turned red as she held out her hand to him.

"Who is that?" I asked sharply, for I didn't like the man.

"That's Dr. Bauerstein," said John shortly.

"And who is Dr. Bauerstein?"

"He's staying in the village for a rest after mental illness. He's one of the greatest living experts on poisons, I believe."

"And he's a great friend of Mary's," put in Cynthia.

John Cavendish asked me to take a walk with him. On our way home again, a pretty young woman came in the opposite direction, bowed and smiled.

"That's a pretty girl," I remarked appreciatively.

John's face hardened.

"That is Mrs. Raikes."

"The one that Eve Howard said Alfred was visiting?"

"Exactly," said John sharply.

I thought of the white-haired old lady in the big house, and that pretty little face that had just smiled into ours, and a vague chill of fear crept over me. I brushed it aside.

"Styles is really a lovely old place," I said to John.

He nodded rather gloomily.

"Yes. It'll be mine someday—should be mine now actually, if my father had only made a decent will. And then I wouldn't be so poor."

"You need money?"

"Yes. I don't mind telling you that I'm broke."

"Couldn't your brother help you?"

"Lawrence? He's gone through every penny he ever had, publishing bad poems in expensive covers. No, we're a careless family with money. My mother's always been awfully good to us, I must say. That is, up to now. Since her marriage, of course—" he broke off, frowning.

For the first time I felt a bad atmosphere. Just for a moment I had a feeling of approaching evil.

Chapter 2—The 16th and 17th of July

The 16th of July fell on a Monday. It was a day of rest following a big party that had taken place on Saturday. I noticed that John seemed very excited and restless.

The following morning, Mrs. Inglethorp suggested Lawrence and I visit Cynthia in the hospital.

Cynthia appeared, looking very cool and cute in her long white coat. She took us up to her office.

"What a lot of bottles!" I cried, as my eye travelled round the small room.

"Say something original," groaned Cynthia.

I laughed

"If you people only knew how fatally easy it is to poison someone by mistake," Cynthia continued, "you wouldn't joke about it. Come on, let's have tea. We've got all sorts of secret stories in that cupboard. No, Lawrence—that's the poison cupboard. The big cupboard—that's right."

We had a very cheery tea, and then Cynthia made a suggestion.

"Come out on our little balcony. You can see all the outside wards there."

I followed Cynthia and her friend and they pointed out the different wards to me. Lawrence remained behind, but after a few moments Cynthia called to him over her shoulder to come and join us. Then she looked at her watch. I guessed it was time to lock up.

As we drove through the village, I remembered that I wanted some stamps, so we pulled up at the post office.

As I came out again, I bumped into a little man who was just entering. He clasped me in his arms and kissed my cheeks.

"*Mon ami* Hastings!" he cried, using the French for 'my friend.'

"Poirot!" I exclaimed.

I turned to the car

"This is a very pleasant meeting for me, Miss Cynthia. This is my old Belgian friend, Monsieur Poirot."

"Oh, we know Monsieur Poirot," said Cynthia brightly. "But I had no idea he was a friend of yours."

I already described Poirot to you at the beginning of my tale, so I won't repeat myself. He pointed out to me the cottage where he lived, and I promised to go and see him soon. Then he raised his hat with a sweep of his hand to Cynthia, and we drove away. "He's a dear little man," said Cynthia. "I'd no idea you knew him."

"You've been friends with a celebrity without knowing it," I replied.

We arrived back in a very cheerful mood. As we entered the hall, Mrs. Inglethorp came out of her boudoir, a small, private room beside the dining room. She looked upset.

"Is there anything the matter, Aunt Emily?" asked Cynthia.

"Certainly not," said Mrs. Inglethorp sharply. "What should there be?" Then catching sight of Dorcas, the maid, going into the dining-room, the old lady told her to bring some stamps into the boudoir.

"Yes, madam." The old servant hesitated, then added shyly: "Don't you think, madam, you'd better go to bed? You're looking very tired."

"Perhaps you're right, Dorcas. No, not now. I've some letters I must finish before the last post goes. Have you lit the fire in my room as I told you?"

"Yes, madam."

"Then I'll go to bed directly after supper."

She went into the boudoir again, and Cynthia stared after her. "Goodness gracious! I wonder what's up?" she said to Lawrence.

He did not seem to have heard her, for without a word he turned on his heel and went out of the house.

I suggested a quick game of tennis before supper and, Cynthia agreeing, I ran upstairs to fetch my racket.

Mary Cavendish was coming down the stairs. It may have been my imagination, but she, too, looked upset.

"Had a good walk with Dr. Bauerstein?" I asked, trying to appear as cool as I could.

"I didn't go," she replied abruptly. "Where is Mrs. Inglethorp?"

"In the boudoir."

She seemed to brace herself for some encounter and went rapidly past me down the stairs across the hall to the boudoir, the door of which she shut behind her.

As I ran out to the tennis court a few moments later, I had to pass the open boudoir window, and was unable to help over-hearing the following bit of dialogue. Mary Cavendish was saying in the voice of a woman desperately controlling herself:

"Then you won't show it to me?"

To which Mrs. Inglethorp replied:

"My dear Mary, it has nothing to do with that thing."

"Then show it to me."

"I tell you it is not what you imagine. It's not about you at all."

To which Mary Cavendish replied bitterly:

"Of course, I might have known you would shield him."

Cynthia was waiting for me, and greeted me eagerly with:

"Wow! There's been the most awful row! Dorcas told me."

"What kind of a row?"

"Between Aunt Emily and *him*. I do hope she's found him out at last!"

"Was Dorcas there, then?"

"Of course not. She 'happened to be near the door'. It was a real bust-up. I do wish I knew what it was all about."

I thought of Mrs. Raikes's pretty face and Eve Howard's warnings but wisely decided to keep quiet whilst Cynthia ex-hausted every possible theory and cheerfully hoped, "Aunt Emily will send Alfred Inglethorp away."

I wanted to find John, but I couldn't see him anywhere. Clearly, something very important had occurred that afternoon. I tried to forget the few words I had overheard; but, try as I might, I could not. What was Mary Cavendish's concern in the matter?

Mr. Inglethorp was in the drawing-room when I came down to supper. His face was as blank as ever.

Mrs. Inglethorp came down last. She still looked upset, and everyone ate, hardy speaking. Mr. Inglethorp never spoke at all. Immediately after supper, Mrs. Inglethorp retired to her boudoir again.

"Send my coffee in here, Mary," she called. "I've just five minutes to catch the last post."

Cynthia and I went and sat by the open window in the draw-ing-room. Mary Cavendish brought our coffee to us. She seemed excited.

"Do you young people want lights, or do you enjoy the evening?" she asked. "Will you take Mrs. Inglethorp her coffee, Cynthia? I will pour it out."

"Don't worry, Mary," said Inglethorp. "I will take it to Emily." He poured it out and went out of the room carrying it carefully.

Lawrence followed him, and Mrs. Cavendish sat down by us. We three sat for some time in silence. It was a glorious night, hot and still. Mrs. Cavendish fanned herself gently with a palm leaf.

"It's almost too hot," she murmured. "We shall have a thunderstorm."

Sadly, these harmonious moments could never endure! My paradise was rudely shattered by the sound of a well-known and disliked voice in the hall.

"Dr. Bauerstein!" exclaimed Cynthia. "What a funny time to come."

I glanced jealously at Mary Cavendish, but she seemed quite calm. In a few moments, Alfred Inglethorp had shown the doctor in. He looked a mess, being totally covered with mud.

"What have you been doing, doctor?" cried Mrs. Cavendish.

"I must make my apologies," said the doctor.

"Well, Bauerstein, you are in a mess," said John, strolling in from the hall. "Have some coffee and tell us what you have been up to."

"Thank you, I will." He laughed and shook his head, as he described how he had discovered a very rare species of fern in a remote place and had lost his footing, slipping into a neighbouring pond.

At this moment, Mrs. Inglethorp called to Cynthia from the hall, and the girl ran out.

"Just carry up my case, will you, dear? I'm going to bed."

The door into the hall was a wide one. I had risen when Cynthia did, John was close by me. There were therefore three witnesses who could swear that Mrs. Inglethorp was carrying her coffee, as yet untasted, in her hand.

My evening was completely spoilt by the presence of Dr. Bauerstein. It seemed to me the man would never go. He rose at last, however, and I breathed a sigh of relief.

"I'll walk down to the village with you," said Mr. Inglethorp. "I must see our solicitor over those estate accounts." He turned to John. "No one need sit up. I will take the front door key."

Chapter 3—The Night of the Tragedy

Here is a plan of the first floor of the Styles Court. The servants' rooms are reached through the door B. They are not allowed in the right wing, where the Inglethorps' rooms were.

It seemed to be the middle of the night when I was awakened by Lawrence Cavendish. He had a candle in his hand, and by the worry on his face I knew that something was seriously wrong.

"What's the matter?" I asked.

"Mother is very ill. She's having some kind of fit. Unfortunately, she has locked herself in."

I sprang out of bed and, pulling on a dressing-gown, followed Lawrence to his mother's bedroom.

John Cavendish joined us, and one or two of the servants were standing around, horrified. Lawrence turned to his brother.

"What should we do?"

John rattled the handle of Mrs. Inglethorp's door violently. It was obviously locked or bolted on the inside. Everyone in the house was up now. The most frightening sounds came from the room.

"Try going through Mr. Inglethorp's room, sir," cried Dorcas.

Suddenly I realized that Alfred Inglethorp was not with us. John opened the door of his room. It was pitch dark, but Lawrence was following with the candle, and by its feeble light we saw that there was no sign of the room having been occupied.

We went straight to the connecting door. That, too, was locked or bolted on the inside.

"Oh, dear, sir," cried Dorcas, wringing her hands, "what ever shall we do?"

"We must try and break the door in, I suppose," John cried. "Tell somebody to go for Dr. Wilkins at once. Now then, we'll have a try at the door. Wait! Isn't there a door into Miss Cynthia's rooms?"

"Yes, sir, but that's always bolted. It's never been undone."

"Well, we might just see."

John ran rapidly down the corridor to Cynthia's room. Mary Cavendish was there, shaking the girl—who must have been a heavy sleeper—and trying to wake her. In a moment or two he was back.

"No good. That's bolted too. We must break in the door. I think this one is a bit less solid than the one in the passage."

We strained and heaved together. The framework of the door was solid, and for a long time it resisted our efforts, but at last we felt it give beneath our weight, and finally, with a loud crash, it was burst open.

We stumbled in together, Lawrence following, still holding his candle. Mrs. Inglethorp was lying on the bed, her whole body stretched in a fit, in one of which she must have overturned the table beside her. Suddenly her limbs relaxed, and she fell back upon the pillows.

John strode across the room and lit the gas light. Turning to Annie, one of the housemaids, he sent her downstairs to the dining-room for brandy. Then he went across to his mother whilst I unbolted the door that opened on the corridor.

I turned to Lawrence. He was white as chalk, the candle he held in his shaking hand was dripping onto the carpet, and his eyes filled with terror as he stared at a point on the further wall. But I could only see the still feebly flickering ashes in the grate, and the neat row of vases on the mantelpiece.

The violence of Mrs. Inglethorp's attack seemed to be passing. She was able to speak in short gasps.

"Better now—very sudden—stupid of me—to lock myself in."

A shadow fell on the bed and, looking up, I saw Mary Cavendish standing near the door with her arm around Cynthia. Her face was heavily flushed, and she yawned repeatedly.

"Poor Cynthia is quite frightened," said Mrs. Cavendish in a low clear voice. She was dressed in her farm smock already. I saw that the clock on the mantelpiece pointed to almost five o'clock.

A strangled cry from the bed startled me. A final fit lifted Emily Inglethorp from the bed, until she appeared to rest upon her head and her heels, with her body arched in a weird manner. Mary and John desperately tried to administer more brandy. The moments flew by. Again, the body arched itself in that weird fashion.

Suddenly Dr. Bauerstein pushed his way into the room. He stopped dead, staring at the figure on the bed, and Mrs. Inglethorp cried out, her eyes fixed on the doctor:

"Alfred—Alfred—" Then she fell back and lay still on the pillows.

The doctor tried to make her breathe. But I think we all knew in our hearts that it was too late. I could see by his face that he had little hope.

Finally, he abandoned his task, shaking his head. At that moment, we heard footsteps outside, and Dr. Wilkins, Mrs. Inglethorp's own doctor, a tubby little man, came in.

In a few words Dr. Bauerstein explained that he had been passing the lodge gates as the car came out and had run up to the house as fast as he could, whilst the car went on to fetch Dr. Wilkins. He pointed to the woman on the bed.

"Her heart was far from strong," murmured Dr. Wilkins. "Poor dear lady."

Dr. Bauerstein, I noticed, was watching the local doctor carefully, as if he didn't trust him.

"I should like to speak to you in private," said Dr. Bauerstein. He turned to John.

We all left the two doctors alone, and I heard the key turned in the lock behind us.

We went slowly down the stairs. I felt terrible. I have a talent for working out clues, and Dr. Bauerstein's manner had started my mind working. Mary Cavendish laid her hand upon my arm.

"What is it? Why did Dr. Bauerstein seem so—peculiar?"

I looked at her and replied.

"Do you know what I think?"

"What?"

"Listen!" I looked round, the others could not hear us. I lowered my voice to a whisper. "I believe she has been poisoned! I'm certain Dr. Bauerstein suspects it."

"*What?*" She shrank against the wall, the pupils of her eyes opening wide. Then, with a sudden cry that startled surprised me, she cried out: "No, no—not that—not that! No, no—leave me. Go down to the others."

I obeyed her, feeling unhappy. John and Lawrence were in the dining-room. I joined them. We were all silent, but I said what we were all wondering when I asked:

"Where is Mr. Inglethorp?"

John shook his head.

"He's not in the house."

Our eyes met. Where *was* Alfred Inglethorp? His absence was strange. I remembered Mrs. Inglethorp's dying words. What did she mean?

At last the doctors came down. Dr. Wilkins spoke to John:

"Mr. Cavendish, I should like your consent to a post-mortem, an operation to examine the body for the cause of death."

"Is that necessary?" asked John seriously. He shut his eyes, as if he felt pain.

"Absolutely," said Dr. Bauerstein.

"Why?"

"Because neither Dr. Wilkins nor myself could give a death certificate until we have done one."

John bent his head.

"In that case, I have no alternative but to agree."

"Thank you," said Dr. Wilkins briskly. "We propose that it should take place tonight. There will be an inquest, an investigation to decide how she died."

Dr. Bauerstein drew two keys from his pocket and told John to lock the room.

The doctors then departed.

"John," I said, "I am going to ask you something."

"Well?"

"You remember my speaking of my friend Poirot? The Belgian who is here? He has been a most famous detective."

"Yes."

"I want you to let me call him in—to investigate this matter."

"What—now? Before the post-mortem?"

"Yes, time is an advantage if—if—there has been a murder."

"Rubbish!" cried Lawrence angrily. "In my opinion the whole thing is Bauerstein's fault! Wilkins didn't think of a post-mortem, until Bauerstein put it into his head. Poisons are his hobby, so of course he sees them everywhere."

I admit that I was surprised by Lawrence's mood. He was so rarely angry about anything.

John hesitated.

"I don't feel like you do, Lawrence," he said at last. "I'm tempted to let Poirot investigate, though I should prefer to wait a bit. We don't want any unnecessary gossip."

"No, no," I cried eagerly, "you don't need to worry about that. Poirot will respect your privacy."

"Very well, then, have it your own way. Though, if it is murder, it seems a clear enough case. God forgive me if I am wronging him!"

I looked at my watch. It was six o'clock. I didn't want to waste time, but I went to the house library and found a medical book, which gave a description of strychnine poisoning.

Chapter 4—Poirot Investigates

I ran to Poirot's house, but stopped when a man came the other way. It was Mr. Inglethorp. Where had he been? He grabbed me and cried:

"My God! This is terrible! My poor wife! I have only just heard."

"Where have you been?" I asked.

"Denby kept me late last night. It was one o'clock before we'd finished. Then I found that I'd forgotten the front door key. I didn't want to wake everyone in the house, so Denby gave me a bed."

"How did you hear the news?" I asked.

"Wilkins knocked on Denby's door to tell him. My poor Emily! Such a kind woman."

A wave of disgust swept over me. What a liar the man was!

"I must hurry on," I said, thankful that he did not ask me where I was bound.

In a few minutes I was knocking at the door of Poirot's cottage. He let me in, and I said that Mrs. Inglethorp had died. I told him of waking up, of Mrs. Inglethorp's dying words, of her husband not being there, of the argument the day before, of the bit of conversation between Mary and her mother-in-law that I had overheard, of the earlier argument between Mrs. Inglethorp and Eve Howard, and of the Eve's whispered message to me.

"You have not told me if Mrs. Inglethorp ate well last night," Poirot replied.

I stared at him. He had to be mad.

"I don't remember," I said. "And, anyway, I don't see—"

"You do not see? But it's very important!"

"I can't see why," I said. "As far as I can remember, she didn't eat much. She was upset."

"Yes," said Poirot thoughtfully, "it was only natural. Excuse me, my friend, you dressed quickly, and your tie is on one side. Allow me." With a skilful movement, he rearranged it.

"That's it! Let's go!"

As we walked quickly, I said:

"Such a sad family now! But if it's a murder, it can't be John or Lawrence."

"She has been kind to these Cavendishes, but remember she was not their own mother. Blood tells—always remember that—blood tells."

"Poirot," I said, "Why did you want to know if Mrs. Inglethorp ate well last night?"

He was silent for a minute or two as we walked along, but finally he said:

"I do not mind telling you—though, as you know, it is not my habit to explain until the end is reached. The present theory is that Mrs. Inglethorp died of strychnine poisoning, taken in her coffee."

"Yes?"

"Well, what time was the coffee served?"

"About eight o'clock."

"That means she drank it between then and half-past eight. Strychnine is a quick poison. Its effects would be felt in about an hour. Yet the symptoms aren't seen until five o'clock the next morning! A big meal might slow its effects. But she ate very little for supper. Strange! Something may be found at the post-mortem to explain it. In the meantime, remember it."

As we neared the house, John came out and met us. He told us that he suspected Alfred Inglethorp.

We went up together to the room of the murder. For convenience I append a plan of the room and furniture in it:

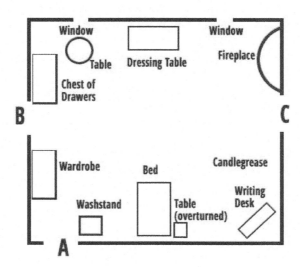

MRS INGLETHORPS BEDROOM
A. — Door into Passage
B. — Door into Mr. Inglethorp's Room
C. — Door into Cynthia's Room

Poirot locked the door on the inside and examined of the room. I stood by the wall and didn't move, making Poirot laugh. I explained that I was afraid of spoiling any footprints.

"Footprints? But what an idea! There has already been practically an army in the room! I will put down my little case until I need it."

He did so, on the round table by the window, but because the top was loose, it collapsed, spilling his case onto the floor.

"Ah, my friend," cried Poirot. "One may live in a big house and yet have no comfort."

After which piece of wisdom, he continued his search.

He took out the key from the lock of a small purple despatch-case on the writing-table and passed it to me. It was an ordinary key with a bit of twisted wire through the handle.

Next, he examined the framework of the door we had broken in, assuring himself that the door had been bolted. Then he went to the door opposite leading into Cynthia's room. That door was also bolted, as I had stated. However, he went to the length of unbolting it, and opening and shutting it several times without making any noise. Suddenly something in the bolt caught his attention. He took out a pair of small tweezers from his case and drew out something tiny, which he carefully sealed up in a tiny envelope.

On the chest of drawers stood a tray with a gas burner and a small saucepan on it. A small amount of a dark fluid remained in the saucepan, and an empty cup and saucer that had been drunk out of stood near it.

I wondered how I could have been so careless as to overlook this. Here was a clue worth having. Poirot delicately dipped his finger into liquid and tasted it cautiously. He frowned.

"Cocoa—with—I think—rum in it."

He passed on to the debris on the floor, where the table by the bed had been overturned. A reading-lamp, some books, matches, a bunch of keys, and the crushed fragments of a coffee-cup lay scattered about.

"Ah, this is curious," said Poirot.

"I admit I see nothing curious about it."

"No? Observe the lamp—the spout is broken in two places; they lie there as they fell. But see, the coffee-cup is absolutely smashed to powder."

"Well," I said, sounding tired, "I suppose someone must have stepped on it."

"Exactly," said Poirot, in an odd voice. "Someone stepped on it."

He rose from his knees, walked slowly across to the mantelpiece and straightened the ornaments there—a habit of his when he was agitated.

"Mon ami," he said, turning to me, "somebody stepped on that cup, grinding it to powder, and the reason they did so was either because it contained strychnine or—which is far more serious—because it did not contain strychnine!"

He picked up the bunch of keys from the floor and twirling them round in his fingers finally selected one, very bright and shining, which he tried in the lock of the purple despatch-case. It fitted opened the box, but after a moment, he closed and re-locked it and slipped the bunch of keys, as well as the key that had originally stood in the lock, into his own pocket.

"Interesting!"

Poirot then searched the drawers of the wash-stand. Crossing the room to the left-hand window, a round stain, hardly visible on the dark brown carpet, seemed to interest him particularly. He went down on his knees, examining it carefully—even smelling it.

Finally, he poured a few drops of the cocoa into a test tube, sealing it up carefully. Then he took out a little notebook.

"We have found in this room," he said, writing busily, "six points of interest. One, a coffee-cup that has been ground into powder; two, a despatch-case with a key in the lock; three, a stain on the floor."

"That may have been done some time ago," I interrupted.

"No, for it is still perceptibly damp and smells of coffee. Four, a fragment of some dark green fabric—only a thread or two, but recognizable."

"Ah!" I cried. "That was what you sealed up in the envelope."

"Yes. Five, this!" With a dramatic gesture, he pointed to a large splash of candle grease on the floor by the writing-table. "It must have been done since yesterday, otherwise a good housemaid would have cleaned it up."

"We probably did it. There was chaos in here."

"You brought only one candle into the room?"

"Yes. Lawrence Cavendish was carrying it. But he was very upset. He seemed to see something over here"—I indicated the mantelpiece—"that absolutely paralysed him."

"That is interesting," said Poirot quickly. "Yes—his eye sweeping the whole length of the wall—but it was not his candle that made this great patch, for you see that this is white grease; whereas Monsieur Lawrence's candle, which is still on the dressing-table, is pink. On the other hand, Mrs. Inglethorp had no candlestick in the room, only a reading-lamp."

"And the sixth point?" I asked. "I suppose it is the sample of cocoa."

"The sixth point I will keep to myself for now."

He looked quickly round the room. "There is nothing more to be done here, I think, unless"—he stared at the dead ashes in the grate. "The fire burns—and it destroys. But by chance—there might be—let us see!"

Carefully, on hands and knees, he began to sort the ashes from the fire, handling them with the greatest caution. Suddenly, he gave a cry.

"The tweezers, Hastings!"

He pulled out a small piece of half charred paper.

"There, mon ami!" he cried. "What do you think of that?"

I looked at the fragment. This is an exact copy of it:

I was puzzled. It was unusually thick, not like ordinary notepaper. Suddenly an idea struck me.

"Poirot!" I cried. "This is a fragment of a will!"

"I expected it."

He put the piece of paper in his case. What was this complication of a will? Who had destroyed it? The person who had left the candle grease on the floor? Obviously. But how had anyone got into the room when the doors were locked? Poirot said:

"Now, I would like to ask a few questions of the maid—Dorcas, her name is, is it not?"

We passed through Alfred Inglethorp's room, and Poirot delayed long enough to make a brief but careful examination of it. We went out through that door, locking both it and that of Mrs. Inglethorp's room as before.

I left him in the boudoir and went to find Dorcas, but when I returned Poirot had stepped into the garden and was admiring flower beds.

"It has been recently done; is it not so?"

"Yes, I believe that the gardeners were at it yesterday afternoon. Dorcas is here."

"Good! Don't hurry me!"

"Yes, but this case is more important."

"And how do you know that the flowers are not equally important?"

Dorcas' grey hair rose in stiff waves under her white cap. She looked at Poirot suspiciously, but he drew forward a chair.

"Take a seat, mademoiselle."

"Thank you, sir."

"You have been with Emily Inglethorp for many years, yes?"

"Ten years, sir."

"That is a long time. You liked her?"

"She was very good to me, sir."

"Then you won't mind my questions."

"Oh, certainly not, sir."

"Let's start with yesterday afternoon. Your mistress had an argument?"

"Yes, sir. But I can't tell you —" Dorcas hesitated.

Poirot looked at her.

"But, naming no names, there's one man in this house that none of us like!"

Poirot waited for her to finish and asked:

"What did you hear of the argument? And what time?"

"About four o'clock. I heard angry voices in here. 'You have lied to me,' Mrs. Inglethorp said. I didn't hear what Mr. Inglethorp replied, but she answered: 'How dare you? My mind is made up. You need not think that any fear of gossip about husband and wife will stop me.' Then I heard them coming out, so I went off quickly."

"Well, what happened next?"

"At five o'clock, Mrs. Inglethorp rang the bell and I took her cup of tea—nothing to eat—to the boudoir. 'Dorcas,' she says, 'I've had a great shock.' She kept staring at something with writing on in her hand. She whispered to herself: 'These few words—and everything's changed.' And then she said to me: 'Never trust a man, Dorcas!' I hurried off."

"What would she do with an important piece of paper afterwards?"

"She would put it in that purple despatch-case, sir. She brought it down with her every morning and took it up every night."

"When did she lose the key of it?"

"Yesterday, lunch-time, sir. She was upset about losing it."

"But she had a duplicate key?"

"Oh, yes, sir."

I wondered why Poirot was so worried about a lost key? He smiled and asked Dorcas.

"Is this the key that was lost?" He drew from his pocket the key that he had found in the lock of the despatch-case upstairs.

Dorcas's eyes looked as though they would pop out of her head.

"That's it, sir. But where did you find it?"

"Ah, but you see it was not in the same place yesterday as it was to-day. Now, did Mrs. Inglethorp have a dark green dress in her wardrobe?"

"No, sir," Dorcas replied, looking startled

"Does anyone else in the house have a green dress?"

"No, sir—not that I know of."

Poirot merely remarked:

"Good, we will leave that and pass on. Was Mrs. Inglethorp likely to take sleeping powder last night?"

"Not last night, sir, I know she didn't."

"Why do you know?"

"Because the box was empty. She took the last one two days ago, and she didn't have any more."

"You are quite sure of that?"

"Positive, sir."

"Then that is cleared up! By the way, Mrs. Inglethorp didn't ask you to sign any paper yesterday?"

"To sign a paper? No, sir."

"When Mr. Hastings and Mr. Lawrence came in yesterday evening, Mrs. Inglethorp was busy writing letters. Do you know to whom these letters were addressed?"

"I'm afraid I couldn't say, sir. I was out in the evening. Perhaps Annie could tell you, though she's a careless girl. Never cleared the coffee-cups away last night."

Poirot lifted his hand.

"Dorcas, leave them a little longer. I should like to examine them."

"Very well, sir."

"What time did you go out last evening?"

"About six o'clock, sir."

"Thank you, Dorcas, that is all I have to ask you." He rose and strolled to the window. "I have been admiring these flower beds. How many gardeners are employed here, by the way?"

"Only three now, sir. Five, we had, before the war. Ah, these are dreadful times!"

"The good times will come again, Dorcas. At least, we hope so. Now, will you send Annie to me here?"

"Yes, sir. Thank you, sir."

"How did you know that Mrs. Inglethorp took sleeping powders?" I asked, as Dorcas left the room. "And about the lost key and the duplicate?"

"As to the sleeping powders, I knew by this."

He suddenly produced a small cardboard box.

"Where did you find it?"

"In the wash-stand drawer in Mrs. Inglethorp's bedroom. It was Number Six of my list of points."

"But I suppose, as the last powder was taken two days ago, it is not of much importance?"

"Probably not, but do you notice anything unusual about this box?"

"No, I can't say that I do."

"The fact that there is no chemist's name?"

"Ah!" I exclaimed. "That is odd!"

"Have you ever known a chemist to send out a box like that, without his printed name?"

"No."

I became quite excited, but Poirot said quickly:

"The explanation is simple, so don't get excited, my friend."

The sound of creaking floorboards announced the approach of Annie.

Poirot said, "About the letters Mrs. Inglethorp wrote last night, Annie. How many were there? And can you tell me any of the names and addresses?"

"There were four letters, sir. One was to Miss Howard, and one was to Mr. Wells, the lawyer, and the other two I don't think I remember, sir—oh, yes, one was to Ross's, the caterers in Tadminster. The other one, I don't remember."

"Think," urged Poirot.

Annie racked her brains in vain. "I'm sorry, sir, but I can't!"

"Never mind," said Poirot. "Now I want to ask you about something else. There is a saucepan in Mrs. Inglethorp's room with some cocoa in it. Did she have that every night?"

"Yes, sir, it was put in her room every evening, and she warmed it up in the night—whenever she fancied it."

"What was it? Plain cocoa?"

"Yes, sir, made with milk, with a teaspoonful of sugar and two teaspoonfuls of rum in it."

"Who took it to her room?"

"I did, sir. I always do. When I draw the curtains, as a rule, sir."

"Did you bring it straight up from the kitchen then?"

"No, sir, you see there's not much room on the gas stove, so cook used to make it early, before putting the vegetables on for supper. Then I used to bring it up, put it on the table by the swing door and take it into her room later."

"What time did you bring it up last night?"

"About quarter-past seven, I should say, sir."

"And when did you take it into Mrs. Inglethorp's room?"

"When I went to shut up, sir. About eight o'clock. Mrs. Inglethorp came up to bed before I'd finished."

"Then, between seven-fifteen and eight o'clock, the cocoa was standing on the table in the left wing?"

"Yes, sir." Annie's face had been growing redder, and now she cried out: "And if there was salt in it, sir, it wasn't me!"

"Salt?" asked Poirot.

"I saw it on the tray, sir. Coarse kitchen salt, it looked. I never noticed it when I took the tray up, but when I came to take it into the mistress's room I saw it at once, so I dusted it off with my apron, and took it in."

I smiled to myself. How Annie would have gasped if she had realized that her "coarse kitchen salt" was strychnine, one of the deadliest poisons known to mankind.

Poirot asked, "When you went into Mrs. Inglethorp's room, was the door leading into Miss Cynthia's room bolted?"

"Oh! Yes, sir; it always was."

"And the door into Mr. Inglethorp's room? Did you notice if that was bolted too?"

"I couldn't say, sir; it was shut, but I couldn't say if it was bolted or not."

"When you left the room, did Mrs. Inglethorp bolt the door after you?"

"No, sir. Probably later. She usually locked it at night."

"Did you notice any candle grease on the floor when you did the room yesterday?"

"Oh, no, sir. Mrs. Inglethorp didn't have a candle, only a reading-lamp."

Then Poirot repeated the question he had put to Dorcas:

"Did your mistress have a green dress?"

"No, sir."

"Nor anyone else in the house?"

Annie reflected.

"No, sir."

"Good! That is all I want to know. Thank you very much."

Annie left the room, making floorboards creak again. My excitement burst out.

"Poirot," I cried, "I congratulate you! This is a great discovery."

"What is a great discovery?"

"That it was the cocoa and not the coffee that was poisoned. That explains why everything! It didn't take effect until the early morning, because the cocoa was only drunk in the middle of the night."

"You think that the cocoa contained strychnine?"

"Of course! What else could the salt on the tray have been?"

"It might have been salt," replied Poirot calmly.

I shrugged my shoulders.

"You are not pleased with me, mon ami?"

"My dear Poirot," I said coldly, "You have a right to your own opinion, just as I have to mine."

"A most admirable sentiment," remarked Poirot. "Whose is the smaller desk in the corner?"

"Mr. Inglethorp's."

"Ah! Locked. But perhaps—" He tried several of Mrs. Inglethorp's keys, twisting and turning them, and finally found one that fitted. "It is not the key, but it works." He opened the desk and saw the neatly filed papers. Then he relocked the desk: "He is a man of method."

A "man of method" was Poirot's highest praise for somebody.

"There were no stamps in his desk, but there might have been, eh, mon ami?"

I felt that my friend was getting old, because he made no sense.

"We're finished here."

Poirot pulled a crumpled envelope out of his pocket and gave it to me. It was a plain, dirty looking old envelope with a few words scrawled across it, apparently at random. Here is a copy of it:

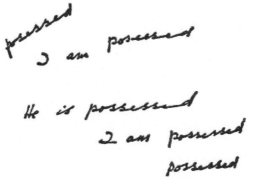

Chapter 5. "It Isn't Strychnine, Is It?"

"Where did you find the envelope?" I asked Poirot.

"In the waste-paper basket. You recognise the handwriting?"

"Yes, it is Mrs. Inglethorp's. But what does it mean?"

Poirot shrugged his shoulders.

A wild idea flashed across me. Was it possible that Mrs. Inglethorp was mad? And, if so, did she take her own life?

Poirot distracted me.

"Let's examine the coffee-cups!"

"What's the point, now that we know about the cocoa?"

"Ah! That stupid cocoa!" cried Poirot.

"And, anyway," I said, coldly, "Since Mrs. Inglethorp took her coffee upstairs with her, we won't find anything, except perhaps a packet of strychnine on the coffee tray!"

Poirot smiled.

"Come, come, my friend," he said, "Allow me my coffee-cups, and I will respect your cocoa. Is it a bargain?"

"Alright!" I laughed.

"You said Mrs. Cavendish stood by the tray—and poured out. Yes. Then she came across to the window where you sat with Mademoiselle Cynthia. Yes. Here are the three cups. And the cup on the mantelpiece, half drunk, that would be Mr. Lawrence Cavendish's. And the one on the tray?"

"John's. I saw him put it down there."

"Good. But where is the cup of Mr. Inglethorp?"

"He does not take coffee."

"Then all are accounted for. Wait!"

With great care, he put a sample from each cup in a separate test tube. He suddenly looked half puzzled and half relieved.

"I had an idea," he said. "But clearly, I was mistaken. Yet it is strange. But no matter!"

"Breakfast is ready," said John Cavendish, coming in from the hall. "May I ask how things are proceeding?" he said. "Was my mother's death natural or murder?"

"Don't be too hopeful" Poirot replied. "What does the rest of the family think?"

"Lawrence says that everything points to its being a simple case of heart failure."

"That is very interesting—very interesting," murmured Poirot softly. "And Mary. Cavendish?"

A faint cloud passed over John's face.

"I don't know what my wife thinks. Hm! Did I tell you that Mr. Inglethorp has returned? It's awkward for all of us. How does one treat a murderer as a normal person?"

Poirot replied:

"I understand. Mr. Inglethorp's reason for not returning last night was, I believe, that he had forgotten the latch-key. Is not that so?"

"Yes."

"What if he did not take it after all?"

"We always keep it in the hall drawer. I could check now?"

"If Mr. Inglethorp did take it, he has had ample time to replace it by now."

"But do you think—"

"I think nothing. If anyone had chanced to look this morning before his return, and seen it there, it would have been a valuable point in his favour. That is all."

John looked confused.

"Let's go and have some breakfast," Poirot said, smiling.

Everyone was assembled in the dining-room. Cynthia looked very tired and ill, I thought. I asked her if she were feeling ill, and she answered:

"Yes, I've got a bad headache."

"Have another cup of coffee, mademoiselle?" said Poirot. "It's very good for headaches." He jumped up and took her cup.

"No sugar," said Cynthia, as he picked up the sugar-tongs.

"No sugar? You abandon it in the war-time, eh?"

"No, I never take it in coffee."

"God!" murmured Poirot to himself, as he brought back the refilled cup.

Only I heard him. I glanced up and saw that his eyes were as green as a cat's. I do not usually call myself dense, but I couldn't think what had changed his mood.

Suddenly, the door opened and Dorcas appeared.

"Mr. Wells to see you, sir," she said to John.

"Show him into my study." Then he turned to us. "My mother's lawyer," he explained. And in a lower voice: "He is also Coroner—so he will organise the inquest. Perhaps you would like to come with me?"

John led us to the study, and I took the moment to whisper to Poirot:

"There will be an inquest then?"

Poirot hardly heard me.

"What is worrying you?" I asked

"Mademoiselle Cynthia does not take sugar in her coffee."

"What?"

"Ah, there is something I do not understand. My instinct was right."

"What instinct?"

"The instinct that made me examine those coffee-cups. Shush! no more now!"

Mr. Wells was a pleasant man with keen eyes and the typical lawyer's mouth. John introduced us.

"I had thought of Friday for the inquest," Mr. Wells said. "That will give us plenty of time for the doctor's report. The post-mortem is to take place to-night, I believe?"

"Yes."

"Can you give us no help in solving it, monsieur?" interrupted Poirot.

"I?"

"Yes, we heard that Mrs. Inglethorp wrote to you last night. You should have received the letter this morning."

"I did, but it just said she wanted my advice on a matter of great importance."

"She gave you no clue as to what that matter might be?"

"That's a great pity," said Poirot, seriously. "Mr. Wells, I would like to ask you something. In the event of Mrs. Inglethorp's death, who would inherit her money?"

"By her last will, dated August of last year, she gave her entire fortune to her stepson, Mr. John Cavendish."

"Was not that—pardon the question, Mr. Cavendish—rather unfair to her other stepson, Mr. Lawrence Cavendish?"

"No, while John would inherit the property, Lawrence, at his stepmother's death, would get a large sum of money."

Poirot nodded thoughtfully.

"I see. But I am right in saying, am I not, that by your English law that will was automatically cancelled when Mrs. Inglethorp remarried?"

"Yes, that document is now cancelled."

"Huh! Was Mrs. Inglethorp herself aware of that fact?"

"She was," said John unexpectedly. "We were discussing the matter of wills being cancelled by marriage only yesterday."

"Ah! One more question, Mr. Wells. You say 'her last will.' Had Mrs. Inglethorp, then, made other wills?"

"She usually made a new will at least once a year," said Mr. Wells.

"Suppose," suggested Poirot, "she had made a new will in favour of Miss Howard—would you be surprised?"

"Not at all."

"Ah!"

Poirot seemed to have exhausted his questions.

"Do you think Mrs. Inglethorp made a will leaving all her money to Miss Howard?" I asked in a low voice, with some curiosity.

Poirot smiled.

"No."

"Then why did you ask?"

"Hush!"

John Cavendish had been talking to Mr. Wells and now turned to Poirot.

"We are going through my mother's papers."

"There *is* a later will." It was Poirot who spoke.

"What?" John and the lawyer looked at him startled.

"Or, rather," pursued my friend imperturbably, "there was one."

"What do you mean—there *was* one? Where is it now?"

"Burnt!" "Burnt?"

"Yes. See here." He took out the charred fragment we had found in the grate in Mrs. Inglethorp's room and handed it to the lawyer with a brief explanation of when and where he had found it.

"But possibly this is an old will?"

"I do not think so. In fact, I am almost certain that it was made no earlier than yesterday afternoon."

"What?"

"Impossible!" broke simultaneously from both men.

Poirot turned to John.

"If you will allow me to send for your gardener, I will prove it to you."

In short, Manning, the gardener came and confirmed that while he and Willum were planting a bed of begonias during the previous afternoon, Mrs. Inglethorp called them in and asked them to sign their names at the bottom of a long paper— under where she'd signed, but she had covered the rest of the paper, so that they never saw what it was about.

"Good heavens!" murmured John, after Manning had left. "That my mother should have made a will on the very day of her death!"

Mr. Wells cleared his throat and remarked drily:

"Are you so sure it is a coincidence, Cavendish?"

"What do you mean?"

"Your mother, you tell me, had a violent quarrel with— someone yesterday afternoon—"

"What do you mean?" cried John again, turning pale.

"After the quarrel your mother hurriedly makes a new will. Then the will disappears. Cavendish, I fear this is no coincidence."

At that moment the loud purr of a car was heard, and we all turned to the window as it swept past.

"Eve!" cried John.

"Excuse me, Wells." He went hurriedly out into the hall.

Poirot looked inquiringly at me.

"Miss Howard," I explained.

"Ah, there is a woman with a head and a heart too, Hastings."

When I saw Miss Howard, I felt guilty. She had known Alfred Inglethorp only too well and asked me to watch him. I wondered whether, if she had remained at Styles, the tragedy would ever have taken place?

I was relieved when she shook me by the hand, with her well-remembered painful grip. But I could see by her red eyes that she had been crying.

"Started the moment I got the news. Just come off night duty. Hired car. Quickest way to get here."

"Have you had anything to eat this morning, Eve?" asked John.

"No."

"I thought not. Come along, breakfast."

"Have they taken him to prison yet?"

"Taken who to prison?"

"Who? Alfred Inglethorp, of course!"

"My dear Eve, do be careful. Lawrence is of the opinion that my mother died from heart seizure."

"More fool, Lawrence!" retorted Miss Howard. "Of course, Alfred Inglethorp murdered poor Emily—as I always told you he would."

"The inquest isn't until Friday."

"Not until fiddlesticks! If he's any sense, he won't stay here and wait to be hanged."

John Cavendish looked at her helplessly.

"Mademoiselle," Poirot said seriously, after we all sat down. "I want to ask you something."

"Ask away."

"I want to be able to count upon your help."

"I'll help you to hang Alfred with pleasure," she replied gruffly. "Hanging's too good for him. Ought to be drawn and quartered, like in good old times."

"I, too, want to hang the criminal."

"Alfred Inglethorp?"

"Him, or another."

"No question of another."

"Believe me, Miss Howard," said Poirot very earnestly, "if Mr. Inglethorp is the man, he shall not escape me. On my honour, I will hang him high!"

"That's better," said Miss Howard.

"But I must ask you to trust me. Now your help may be very valuable to me. I will tell you why. Because, in all this house of mourning, yours are the only eyes that have wept."

Miss Howard blinked, and a new note crept into the gruffness of her voice.

"I was fond of her. I watched over her. I guarded her from the lot of them, and then a crook comes along, and pah! all my years of caring gone."

"I understand, mademoiselle. You think that we are cold, but trust me, it is not so."

John stuck his head in and invited us both to come up to Mrs. Inglethorp's room, because he and Mr. Wells had finished looking through the desk in the boudoir.

"You've got the keys still, haven't you, Poirot?" I asked, as we reached the door of the locked room.

Taking the keys from Poirot, John unlocked it, and we all passed in.

"My mother kept most of her important papers in this despatch-case, I believe," he said.

"Permit me," Poirot said. "I locked it this morning."

"But it's not locked now."

"Impossible!"

"See." And John lifted the lid as he spoke.

"Thundering Thanatos!" cried Poirot. "And I—who have both the keys in my pocket! This lock has been forced."

"What?"

Poirot laid down the case again.

"But who forced it? Why should they? When? But the door was locked?"

Poirot answered them categorically—almost mechanically.

"Who? That is the question. Why? Ah, if I only knew. When? Since I was here an hour ago. As to the door being locked, it is a very ordinary lock. Probably any other key to a door in this passage would fit it."

We stared at one another blankly. Poirot had walked over to the mantelpiece. He was outwardly calm, but I noticed his hands, which were straightening the spill vases on the mantelpiece, were shaking.

"It was like this," he said at last. "There was something in that case—some piece of evidence, slight in itself perhaps, but still enough of a clue to connect the murderer with the crime. Therefore, he took the risk, the great risk, of coming in here and forcing the lock."

"But what was it?"

"Ah!" cried Poirot, with a gesture of anger. "That, I do not know! A document of some kind, without doubt, possibly the scrap of paper Dorcas saw in her hand yesterday afternoon. I should have carried it away with me. And now it is destroyed—but is it destroyed? We must leave no stone unturned."

He rushed like a madman from the room. I followed, but by the time I had reached the top of the stairs, he was out of sight.

Mary Cavendish stood where the staircase branched, staring down into the hall.

"What has happened to your amazing little friend, Mr. Hastings? He has just rushed past me like a mad bull."

"He's rather upset about something," I replied.

I could hear Poirot shouting. The little man appeared to be telling the whole household everything. Once again, I could not help regretting that my friend was going mad. I stepped briskly down the stairs. The sight of me calmed Poirot almost immediately. I drew him aside.

"My dear fellow," I said, "is this wise? Surely you don't want the whole house to know about the lost paper? You are actually playing into the criminal's hands."

"You think so, Hastings?"

"I am sure of it."

"Well, well, my friend, I will be guided by you. Let us go. Come with me to the village."

On the way we saw Cynthia, to whom Poirot addressed a question:

"Did you ever make up Mrs. Inglethorp's medicines?"

A slight flush rose in her face, as she answered:

"No."

"Only her powders?"

The flush deepened as Cynthia replied:

"Oh, yes, I did make up some sleeping powders for her once."

"These?" Poirot produced the empty box which had contained powders.

She nodded.

"Can you tell me what they were? Sulphonal? Veronal?"

"No, they were bromide powders."

"Ah! Thank you, mademoiselle; good morning."

As we walked briskly away from the house, I glanced at him more than once. I had often before noticed that, if anything excited him, his eyes turned green like a cat's. They were shining like emeralds now.

"My friend," he broke out at last, "I have a little idea, a very strange, and probably impossible idea. And yet—it fits in."

I shrugged my shoulders. I privately thought that Poirot was letting his imagination take control. In this case, surely, the truth was only too plain and apparent.

"So that is the explanation of the blank label on the box," I said. "Very simple. I'm amazed I did not think of it myself. Tell me, how did those scribbled words on the envelope help you to discover that a will was made yesterday afternoon?"

Poirot smiled.

"Mon ami, haven't you ever tried a word once or twice on a scrap of paper, to see if it looked right? Well, that is what Mrs. Inglethorp did. Now, 'possessed' is a word used often in wills. This was confirmed by something else. Near the desk were several traces of brown mould and earth. I learnt from you that begonia beds had been planted yesterday afternoon. Thus, the gardeners had come into the room and signed a new will."

"That was very clever," I could not help admitting.

He smiled.

"You gave too much rein to your imagination. Imagination is a good servant, and a bad master. The simplest explanation is always the most likely."

"Another point—how did you know that the key of the despatch-case had been lost?"

"I guessed it. You saw that it had a piece of twisted wire through the handle, suggesting it had been pulled off of a flimsy key-ring. Now, if it had been lost and recovered, Mrs. Inglethorp would have replaced it on her bunch; but on her bunch I found what was obviously the duplicate key, very new and bright, which led me to guess that somebody else had inserted the original key in the lock of the despatch-case."

"Yes," I said, "Alfred Inglethorp, without doubt."

Poirot looked at me curiously.

"You are very sure of his guilt?"

"Well, naturally. Every fresh circumstance seems to establish it more clearly."

"The opposite is true," said Poirot quietly, "there are several points in his favour."

"Oh, come now!"

"Yes."

"I see only one."

"And that?"

"That he was not in the house last night."

"'Bad shot!' as you English say! You have chosen the one point that is against him."

"How?"

"Because if Mr. Inglethorp knew that his wife would be poisoned last night, he would certainly have made up an excuse to be away from the house. That leaves us two possibilities: either he knew what was going to happen or he had a reason of his own for his absence."

"And that reason?" I asked sceptically.

Poirot shrugged his shoulders.

"This Mr. Inglethorp, I should say, is somewhat of a crook—but that does not of necessity make him a murderer."

I shook my head, unconvinced.

"We do not agree, eh?" said Poirot. "Let's agree to disagree. What do you make of the fact that all the doors of the bedroom were bolted on the inside?"

"Well—" I considered. "One must look at it logically."

"True."

"I would put it this way. The doors were bolted—our own eyes have told us that—yet the presence of the candle grease on the floor, and the burning of the will, prove that during the night someone entered the room. You agree so far?"

"Perfectly."

"Well," I said, encouraged, "as the person who entered did not do so by the window, nor by miraculous means, it follows that the door must have been opened from inside by Mrs. Inglethorp herself. She would naturally open the door to her own husband, so it had to be him."

Poirot shook his head.

"Why should she? She had bolted the door leading into his room and had had a quarrel with him that very afternoon. No, he was the last person she would allow in."

"But you agree with me that the door must have been opened by Mrs. Inglethorp herself?"

"There is another possibility. She may have forgotten to bolt the door into the passage when she went to bed and locked it later."

"Poirot, are you serious?"

"No, I do not say it is so, but it might be. Now, to turn to another feature, what do you make of the scrap of conversation you overheard between Mrs. Cavendish and her mother-in-law?"

"I had forgotten. That is as confusing as ever. It seems incredible that a woman like Mrs. Cavendish should interfere so much in what was not her business."

"Exactly. It was an amazing thing for a woman like her to do."

"Still, it is unimportant, and need not be taken into account."

A groan burst from Poirot.

"What have I always told you? Everything must be taken into account. If the fact will not fit the theory—let the theory go."

"Well, we shall see," I said, irritated.

"Yes, we shall see."

We had reached his cottage, where he set up two chairs by the window.

"Look, Poirot!" I said.

He leant forward.

"Lord!" he said. "It is Mr. Mace, from the chemist's shop. He is coming here." The young man stopped next to the cottage, and, after hesitating, banged on the door. I followed Poirot as he went to answer.

"Oh, Mr. Poirot, I'm sorry for coming. It's all over the village about old Mrs. Inglethorp dying so suddenly. They do say—" he lowered his voice cautiously—"that it's poison?"

Poirot's face remained quite calm.

"Only the doctors can tell us that, Mr. Mace."

"Yes, exactly—of course—" Mr. Mace suddenly clutched Poirot by the arm, and sank his voice to a whisper: "Just tell me this, Mr. Poirot, it isn't—it isn't strychnine, is it?"

Poirot gave a vague answer and Mr. Mace left.

"Yes," he said to me, nodding seriously. "He will have evidence to give at the inquest."

We went slowly upstairs again. I was opening my lips, when Poirot stopped me with a gesture of his hand.

"Not now, not now, mon ami. My mind is in some disorder—which is not good."

He sat still for ten minutes. At last he heaved a deep sigh.

"It is good. The bad moment has passed. Now all is organised. One must never permit confusion. The case is not clear yet—no. For it is very complicated! It puzzles me. Me, Hercule Poirot! There are two, important facts."

"And what are they?"

"The first is the weather yesterday."

"Poirot, you're teasing me!"

"No. The thermometer said 80 degrees in the shade. Do not forget that, my friend. It is the key to the whole riddle!"

"And the second point?" I asked.

"The fact that Monsieur Inglethorp wears very peculiar clothes, has a black beard and uses glasses."

"Are you serious?"

"I am absolutely serious, my friend."

"But this is childish!"

"No, it is very important."

"And supposing the Coroner's jury returns a verdict of Wilful Murder against Alfred Inglethorp. What becomes of your theories, then?"

"I would not allow it." Tears came into his eyes. "That Mrs. Inglethorp was very good to us Belgians. She would never forgive me if I let her husband be arrested *now*—when a word from me could save him."

Cynthia's Hospital

Chapter 6—The Inquest

In the interval before the inquest, Poirot was busy. Twice he visited Mr. Wells. He also took long walks into the country, alone. I was upset that he hadn't taken me, because I wanted to understand his theory on the case.

It occurred to me that he might have been making inquiries at Raikes's farm, so I made my way there. Sitting on a wall was an old man, who grinned at me with a toothless smile. In short, I asked him if there had been any gentlemen visitors from Styles, and he assured me that there had been one, so I knew that Eve Howard had been right about Alfred Inglethorp. The thought disgusted me. Such an old man and young lady!

On one point, Poirot had been troubled. He repeatedly asked Dorcas if the quarrel had been at four-thirty and not four, as she had said, but she insisted that it had been four.

The inquest on Friday was a short affair. The poison specialist, Dr. Bauerstein, confirmed that the poison could not have been taken by mistake and that he knew it had not been put in the cocoa, because he had had it tested. He also confirmed that Poirot had thought; that the strychnine could not have been put in the coffee, because its effect didn't occur until many hours later. In short, he had no idea how the poison had been given. He also said that strychnine's taste was so bitter that cocoa would not have disguised its taste but that coffee might. Dr. Wilkins agreed on all points, but asserted that it could not have been suicide, because he knew Mrs. Inglethorp to be a woman of strong spirit.

Lawrence came next and said nothing important until he suggested that the death could have been accidental, because Mrs. Inglethorp had been taking medicine that contained strychnine for some time. But Dr. Wilkins laughed at the idea, saying that even the cumulative effect of such a tiny dose of strychnine would be so small that Mrs. Inglethorp would have had to drink the whole bottle in one go to kill herself.

Mary Cavendish came next. She was asked what she remembered of the quarrel that she overheard. It seemed to me that she hesitated a lot, making me believe that she was playing for time. When she did reply, she only confirmed what Dorcas had said; that Mrs. Inglethorp had said something about, "Causing gossip about husband and wife."

The Coroner finished questioning Mary, though he seemed dissatisfied. I, myself, thought she was hiding something.

The two gardeners confirmed that they had signed a piece of paper in Mrs. Inglethorp's room.

Eve Howard produced the letter sent to her by Mrs. Inglethorp on the 17th. It read:

> Styles Court, Essex
> Handwritten note.
> July 17th
> My dear Eve,
> Can we forget our disagreement? I have found it
> hard to forgive the things you said against my dear
> husband, but I am an old woman & very fond of
> you.
> Yours affectionately,
> Emily Inglethorp

The jury looked at the letter and the Coroner said that it didn't help much.

"Plain as a pikestaff to me!" Eve Howard said. "Alfred did it!"

"We can't say that!" the Coroner replied.

Then the chemist's assistant, Mr. Mace. He looked embarrassed an admitted selling strychnine to Alfred Inglebrook without permission, which was against the law. When asked why he did it, he said that Mr. Inglebrook had told him a dog needed to be put to sleep, and because Alfred was the richest man in the area, he didn't want to say no—after all, the Inglebrook's didn't normally come to this chemist, and if they switched, it would help the business. However, Mr. Mace *had* made Alfred leave his signature in a book, and he displayed it.

Mr. Inglebrook was called, and the jury hushed. He denied visiting Mr. Mace's chemist and said that there was no dog at Styles. When asked where he was on the evening of 16th July he said he couldn't remember, except that he was out walking and didn't see anybody.

Poirot became angry and whispered to me:

"He is stupid! Does he *want* to be arrested?"

The Coroner then asked about the quarrel on the afternoon of Tuesday.

"Pardon me. I had no argument with my wife that day. I wasn't even there!"

"Do you have a witness?"

"You have my word."

"Did you take the coffee to your wife that evening?"

"No, I was going to, but I had to do something, so I left it in the hall."

"How do you explain your wife calling your name twice, just before she died."

"The room was poorly lit. Perhaps she mistook my stepson for me."

Poirot chuckled at the clever reply.

"Furthermore," Mr. Inglebrook said, "her cries of my name were not an accusation but an appeal! She wanted my help!"

The jury gasped at his boldness.

At this point I noticed two men at the back of the room. I asked Poirot who they were.

"That little man is Detective Inspector James Japp of Scotland Yard. The other man is from there too."

Rolls Royce

Chapter 7—Poirot Pays His Debt

Outside the courtroom, Poirot held me back and introduced me to Japp, with whom he had had a professional friendship some years before. The other man, Summerhaye, seemed friendly enough, but both agreed that the case was clear against Alfred Inglebrook. Indeed, they were on their way to Styles Court, where they would arrest him after a short investigation and search of their own.

"But you can't arrest him! Not yet!" Poirot said.

Summerhaye became angry, but Japp held him back, saying:

"If Poirot says there is more to this, I would like to hear, because I don't want to make a mistake. We are just visiting the doctor and Coroner, before we go to the house. May we call on you?"

Poirot gave them directions to his cottage and told me that he thought Alfred Inglebrook was innocent.

"But the evidence against him is complete!" I argued.

"Yes, too complete! Real evidence is usually vague and hard to find. Look at it like this; a man has lived by his wits. He sets out to murder his wife, and yet he has no story prepared, and the evidence against him is complete. Does that make sense to you, mon ami?"

"But—"

"And on top of this, the chemist, Mr. Mace identified him! No"

"So how do you explain it?"

"He didn't buy the strychnine."

"He didn't? But—"

"Mr. Mace said he didn't know Mr. Inglebrook well. Therefore, he might not have looked too closely when he saw the beard and glasses. Remember the second point I told you was most important in this case?"

"That Mr. Inglebrook wears unusual clothes, has a black beard and glasses?"

"Yes!"

"You think it was somebody in disguise?"

"Exactly, mon ami!"

"But then why won't he say where he was at six o'clock on Monday evening?"

"If he was arrested, he would say. But I don't want that. Did anything about the inquest seem strange to you?"

I thought of Mary Cavendish, but I didn't want to say.

"It hadn't occurred to me before," Poirot continued, "but why would Dr. Bauerstein be up and walking so early in the morning?"

"I heard he has trouble sleeping—"

"Ah! But that is too vague. We must keep an eye on him. One thing I know now; Dorcas was correct. She did hear the quarrel at four, as she said. I was wrong about something. But there is something else. Two witnesses were not telling the truth. But I am not thinking of Mr. Inglebrook."

"Then who could it be? Surely not Mary Cavendish or Lawrence? That only leaves John, Cynthia and Eve Howard."

"I do not believe that Cynthia is such a heavy sleeper that she heard nothing. But leave that aside."

"Then Eve Howard? But she seems too honest!"

But at that moment Japp and Summerhaye arrived. Japp asked:

"We are going to Styles. Will you both accompany us?"

At the house, Japp gathered everyone together.

"Mr. Inglebrook," Poirot began, "I don't think you realise the danger you are in."

"My poor wife! What do you mean; danger?"

"There is a lot of evidence against you."

"What do you mean?"

"You are suspected of poisoning your wife."

"You must tell us where you were at six o'clock on Monday evening."

Alfred Inglethorp groaned and put his head in his hands.

"Speak!" Poirot said, angrily.

"No!"

"Then I speak for you! Mr. Inglethorp was escorting the farmer's wife, Mrs. Raikes, home at six o'clock on Monday evening. I have five witnesses who will swear it! There is no doubt that Mr. Inglethorp did not murder his wife!"

Chapter 8—Fresh Suspicions

"Can you give us the list of witnesses?" Japp said, astonished.

"Of course."

"So Mr. Inglethorp wouldn't say where he was, because he wanted to protect the reputation of his wife?"

"Yes."

"I was foolish, no doubt," said Mr. Inglebrook, jumping up. "But you can never know how unfairly I have been treated!" He threw a glance at Eve Howard.

The meeting ended and Poirot showed Japp all the evidence. Then he took me upstairs and made me wait by the swing door in the left wing.

"Wait her until I come for you," he told me.

He didn't come for twenty minutes, by which time I had begun to wonder if I was supposed to catch somebody.

"What was that about?" I asked him.

"Did you hear anything?"

"Nothing."

"Not a bump?"

"No."

"I knocked over the table in Mrs. Inglebrook's room, and you didn't hear it. Interesting!"

Just then I happened to glance out of the window.

"Dr. Bauerstein is coming up the driveway. He's a clever man."

"Yes, very clever."

"You should have seen him on Tuesday. Covered in mud, he was!"

"What?" Poirot cried, grabbing me by my shoulders. "He was here? And you never told me? Why? Why?"

Poirot seemed to go into a frenzy.

"Is it important?" I asked.

"It changes everything! Everything! We must act at once. Where is Mr. Cavendish? I need to borrow his car and go to Tadminster."

"But what is wrong?"

"Now we know that Mr. Inglebrook didn't do it, but we must find out who took the coffee to his wife. It's vital we find out. We know it wasn't Mrs Cavendish or Cynthia. But it could be anybody else. I have had to reveal my theory too soon. Now the murderer will be cautious! He, or she, will be harder to catch. Do you have an idea who it is?"

"No. Well, perhaps, but it is mad!"

"Tell me?"

"Eve Howard! Her anger against Mr. Inglebrook just seems unnatural. Do we know she wasn't here the night of the murder? She lives only fifteen miles away."

"Yes. I checked. A convoy came through, so she had to remain all night on duty in the hospital."

"Oh. Then it can't be her. After all, she was so good to Mrs. Inglebrook."

"Tch! You are like a child. If she could murder the woman, she could certainly act as if she was good to her. But there is a problem with Miss Howard as a suspect."

"What?"

"She would not benefit from the murder."

"What if Mrs. Inglebrook made a will out in her favour?"

"No. She didn't."

"Then let's find Eve Howard innocent!"

"Hm. I want you to do something for me. Next time you are alone with Lawrence, I want you to say this, 'I have a message from Poirot; find the extra coffee-cup and you can rest in peace.' Nothing more. Nothing less."

I repeated the message, feeling mystified.

"What does it mean?" I asked.

"You will find out."

By now, we were arriving in Tadminster, in John's car. Poirot stopped outside the "Analytical Chemist" and disappeared inside for two minutes. When he climbed back into the car, he looked pleased with himself.

"What did you do?" I asked.

"I left a sample of the cocoa to be tested, mon ami."

"But it already has been tested."

"By who?"

"Dr. Bauerstein."

"Of course. And do we trust him?"

"No."

I had started to trust Poirot's judgement after he had proved Mr. Inglebrook innocent, so I let it go.

The funeral took place the following day, and on Monday John drew me aside at breakfast and told me that Mr. Inglebrook was leaving.

"He's going to live in the Stylites Arms pub until his affairs are settled. Of course, we feel bad about him going, now that we know he's innocent. But it's very awkward having him here."

"I see. Will you have enough money to look after the place now?"

"Oh yes. Things will be alright now."

The newspapers were full of articles about the murder that morning. It was terrible for the family. I read a few articles and then stood up to leave. But the maid, Dorcas, pulled me aside.

"I have something for Mr. Poirot, sir," she said. "You know he asked me about the green dress?"

"You found one?"

"No, sir, but I remembered that the boys used to dress up with clothes from a chest in the attic. It's still there, and there may be a green dress in that, sir."

"Thank you very much Dorcas. I will tell Poirot at once."

I started out for the village, but encountered Poirot, coming the other way. I told him about the chest, and he led me straight to the attic. He had almost emptied out all its contents, old clothes of every type and description, when he held up something black and cried:

"Aha!" It was a black beard. "New! Yes, quite new!"

After a moment's hesitation, he led me downstairs to find Dorcas. She was polishing the silver.

"Dorcas, did the boys often play with clothes from the chest?"

"Yes, when they were children. But not so often now. Occasionally they dress up for a play. Only recently, Lawrence dressed up as the Shah of Persia and Miss Cynthia was an apache Indian."

"Hm. Did Lawrence wear a beard when he played the Shah?"

"Yes, he did, but only an old thing I knitted for him many years ago. It looks good from far away."

Poirot led me back to the hall, but I couldn't help asking:

"Do you think it's the one?"

"Did you notice it had been trimmed?"

"Yes, it was cut exactly the same shape as Mr. Inglebrook's. I wonder who put it there?"

"He was somebody with great intelligence. We must be clever to catch him! Yes, very clever. So clever that he will think we are not clever at all! There, mon ami, you can be of great help."

"Me?"

I was very pleased that Poirot had at least realised my worth.

"I must have an ally in the house," Poirot added. "Somebody we can trust."

"You have me?"

"Somebody who is not working on the case."

"Oh."

"Ah! Here comes Eve Howard. She's just the right person! Hello Miss Howard."

"You didn't hang him!"

"Miss Howard. I need your help to catch the real suspect."

"I still think it's Mr. Inglebrook!"

"Miss Howard, the reason you so strongly think this, is because you don't want to believe who you think, in your heart, really did it. You know who I mean!"

"No! No! No!"

"You know it. Your instinct tells you."

"No. I don't know what put such a wild—such a dreadful idea into my head!"

"I am right, am I not?" asked Poirot.

"Yes, yes; but you must have been a wizard to have guessed. It can't be so. It's impossible! Don't ask me for help. I won't! I won't!"

Poirot nodded as if satisfied and replied:

"You will help me, despite yourself. I will ask you nothing. I only need you as an ally. You will do one thing for me."

"And what is that?"

"Watch."

"Yes, I can't help that. I am always watching."

"Good. And let's hope we are wrong. But if we're right, then whose side are you on?"

"Oh, I don't know! It could be hushed up!"

"No. It must not be. Miss Howard, this is unworthy of you."

"Yes, she was a dear soul."

"Then we are agreed?"

Miss Howard only gave the slightest nod, before turning and walking away in tears.

"You both seem to agree about who it is," I whispered. "Will you tell me?"

"No. Two is enough for a secret."

Chapter 9—Dr. Bauerstein

Until now I had no chance to deliver my message to Lawrence Cavendish. I found him in the garden and moved close to him.

"I have a message for you from Poirot."

"What is it?"

"Find the extra coffee-cup and you can rest in peace."

"What does he mean?"

"I don't know. I was hoping you could tell me?"

"I have no idea. If he wants to know about coffee cups, he should speak to Dorcas."

Poirot was invited to lunch, but we all agreed not to talk about the affair, that is, until the little Belgian detective turned to Mary Cavendish and asked:

"Mademoiselle, was the door bolted on Cynthia's side of Mrs. Inglebrook's when you entered?"

"Yes. Locked."

"No, I said bolted."

"Ah, I didn't notice."

"But I did!" Lawrence cut in. "It *was* bolted."

"Ah, that settles it then."

I felt happy, that for once Poirot's idea had come to nothing, whatever it was.

I decided, there and then, to visit Dr. Bauerstein. Somebody had to keep an eye on him. But when I knocked on his door a woman answered.

"He's not here," she said. "The police arrested him."

Chapter 10—The Arrest

Arriving at Poirot's cottage I knocked on the door to tell him the news. But I found out from another Belgian that he had gone to London. Annoyed, I went home and stewed, not knowing what to do without my friend. The following morning, I read the newspapers keenly, expecting news of the arrest. But there was none. I set off for Poirot's cottage again but met the detective coming the other way.

"Poirot! Thank god. I Didn't know what to do! I haven't spoken to anybody except John about it. Is that right?"

"About what? What is wrong?"

"The arrest of Bauerstein."

"They arrested him?"

"Didn't you know?"

"Well it makes sense. We're only five miles from the coast."

"What are you talking about?"

"He's probably been arrested for spying, mon ami, not the murder!"

"He's a spy?"

"Didn't you suspect it? Why else would an important doctor from London come to live in the country? And why would he be walking around late at night?"

"I hadn't thought of that. Then he doesn't love Mary after all!"

"No, and I don't think she cares about him. She cares about somebody else."

"Do you think so?"

I was so flattered that I couldn't find anything to say while we walked back to the house.

Eve Howard walked straight up to Poirot, handed him a sheet of brown paper and said:

"On top of the wardrobe."

With that, she turned away.

Poirot read a few words on the brown paper and pocketed it without sharing their meaning.

Poirot did not make an appearance the following morning and nor did the Scotland Yard men. But at lunchtime we finally found out where the fourth letter had gone. We received a reply from a music publisher in London thanking Mrs. Inglebrook for her cheque and informing her that they had been unable to trace a series of Russian folk songs.

I strolled down to Poirot's cottage after lunch but found, to my annoyance, that he wasn't home. When I asked if he had gone to London, I was told he had gone to visit a young lady's pharmacy in Tadminster. I asked for his Belgian friend to tell Poirot to call on us the following day, but he still didn't come.

I was sulking in the garden when Lawrence found me. He whispered:

"I found the extra coffee-cup."

I told Lawrence not to talk to anybody and left him to find Poirot. To my relief he was at home but sitting at a table with his head in his hands.

"What is wrong?" I asked him.

"Wrong? Nothing. But I have to decide something of great importance. The most serious of all things hangs in the balance."

"What is that?"

"A woman's happiness, mon ami," he said seriously. "I don't know what to do. For I play for a big stake. Nobody except I, Hercule Poirot would attempt it."

Confused, I tried a simpler subject:

"Lawrence has found the coffee-cup."

"Ah! He is cleverer than I thought."

I told him off for visiting Cynthia on a day when she was working, but he only replied that another lady had shown him all he wanted to see. I also told him about the letter from the music publisher, but Poirot merely waved the news away.

"It is of no important, mon ami." With a sigh he stood up and said, "I want you to look at these." He laid three photographs on the table. "I have labelled them 1, 2, 3."

"Fingerprints! No. 1 I would say is a man's, thumb and first finger. No. 2 is a lady's, much smaller. No. 3—" I paused. "Lots of confused fingerprints, but these are No. 1's."

"Are you sure?"

"Yes. I suppose that as usual you are not going to explain?"

"On the contrary, No. 1 were fingerprints of Monsieur Lawrence. No. 2 were those of Madamoiselle Cynthia. No. 3 are more complicated. But I only obtained them for comparison. Do you want to know where I found them?"

"Yes please!"

"On a bottle in Madamoiselle Cynthia's pharmacy."

"But that is impossible. Lawrence was with us all the time!"

"That is not so. You told me yourself you went out onto the balcony."

"Only for a few seconds."

"But it was long enough for a man who once studied medicine to satisfy his curiosity."

"Poirot, what was in that bottle?"

"Hydro chloride of strychnine."

"Good heavens."

"This particular type of strychnine preserves fingerprints. Otherwise I couldn't have photographed them."

"How did you do it anyway?"

"I dropped my hat from the balcony! While Mademoiselle Cynthia's friend went to fetch it—"

"Then you suspected Lawrence?"

"I don't know. But there is far too much strychnine in this case, mon ami; strychnine obtained from Mr. Mace, in Mrs. Inglebrook's medicine. And now this! Let us go now to the house."

But when we arrived Dorcas came running out to meet us.

"Oh, Mr. Hastings. They have arrested John!"

I turned just in time to see a look of victory in Poirot's eyes.

Poirot's Cottage

Chapter 11—The Case For The Prosecution

John's trial took place two months later. Mary Cavendish stood by his side, fighting every inch of the way to prove his innocence.

At the trial, I spoke with Poirot.

"Mary proved to be loyal to her husband after all!" I whispered.

"She thinks of nothing but him."

I suddenly realised that Mary was the woman, for whose happiness Poirot fought. I was glad the decision had been taken out of his hands.

"But John! My old friend!" I said.

"Every murderer is somebody's old friend. You cannot mix up emotion and logic."

"You could have given me a hint."

"I didn't, because he *was* your old friend."

"Do you think he will be found guilty?"

"The opposite is true. I think he will be found innocent. You see, there is so little evidence. And I, Hercule Poirot, lack the last link, the last piece of the puzzle."

"When did you know?"

"Did you not wonder who could have argued with Mrs. Inglebrook, if not her husband? It could only have been either Lawrence or John. But if it was Lawrence, Mary Cavendish's behaviour would not have made sense."

"Hm."

"But there is something important. I cannot appear at the trial. I must stay hidden. I must be seen to be working for John's defence, not his prosecution."

"But why?"

"It takes a great deal of intelligence to catch a very clever man, mon ami. Japp made all the discoveries, and he will take all the credit. Strangely enough, I can give evidence to bring down one point of the prosecution."

"What's that?"

"John did not destroy the will."

September found us all in London, staying in a large house that Mary had rented. I had a new job at the War Office, so I could see them at weekends. As the weeks went by Poirot seemed more and more depressed. He could not find the missing link. I hoped he never would, because I didn't want Mary to be unhappy.

On the 15th the trial took place. Much of it was just like the earlier inquest, but some new facts came out. Firstly, a tube of strychnine had been found by Japp in John's room. This tube was identified by the chemist as the same one he thought he had sold to Mr. Inglebrook. Secondly, a parcel had arrived from Parkson's Theatrical Costumes. Neither Dorcas not Eve Howard remembered it, but Miss Howard admitted under questioning that it was she that had found the brown paper parcel. She eventually admitted that she had found it on the top of John Cavendish's wardrobe. Paperwork from Parkson's revealed that a black beard had been sent to Lawrence Cavendish at Styles Court.

Elizabeth Wells, second maid at Styles, said that she had locked the front door, instead of leaving it on the latch, as Mr. Inglebrook had asked, and gone back downstairs later to correct her mistake. She had heard a noise in the West Wing, peeped along the passage and saw John Cavendish knock on Mrs. Inglebrook's door.

Mr. Japp was called by the prosecution. He revealed that new evidence had been found. A piece of blotting paper found in Mrs. Inglebrook's chequebook, when reversed in a mirror, revealed the words, " … erything of which I die possessed I leave to my husband Alfred Ing … " Japp then produced the charred bit of thick will paper, and this, with the discovery of the beard in the attic completed his evidence.

More evidence came on the following day. John had been in financial difficulties but had found time to begin an affair with Mrs. Raikes, the farmer's wife. I felt sorry for Mary.

Lawrence, of course, denied ordering the beard.

There was little other evidence. Handwriting experts examined the signature on the prescription for strychnine from the chemist and concluded that it wasn't Alfred Inglebrook's. They also asserted that it could have been that of the prisoner.

I visited Poirot in his room that night. He was very unhappy and spent his time building a house from a pack of playing cards. I was amazed at how steady his hand was as the house rose higher and higher, each card placed exactly in the correct position.

"Your hand is so steady!" I said.

"Not always."

"I've only seen your hand shake once!"

"When I was angry, I suppose."

"Yes, when you discovered Mrs. Inglebrook's case had been forced open. You twiddled with the things on the mantelpiece, as you often do, and your hand shook like a leaf!"

Poirot let out a terrible cry and covered his eyes with his hands.

"Are you alright?" I asked, worried.

"Yes! I have an idea! A really big idea! And you gave it to me."

He stood up, kissed me on both cheeks and ran from the room. He left the house, crying out, "A car! I need a car!"

When night fell, he still hadn't returned.

Chapter 12—The Last Link

Poirot still hadn't returned by lunchtime the next day, a Sunday. But at three o'clock he arrived in a car with Japp and Summerhaye, looking very pleased with himself. He gathered everyone in the lounge, including Dorcas, Miss Howard and Mr. Inglebrook, to whom he had sent a note earlier.

Poirot began by explaining:

"I was asked to investigate this case by John Cavendish. I at once examined Mrs. Inglebrook's room and found a fragment of green cloth, a stain on the carpet, still wet, and an empty box of bromide powders. I found the green material in the bolt of the door between Mademoiselle Cynthia room and Mrs. Inglebrook's. The police didn't recognise what it was; a piece torn from the arm of a green land smock. Now, there is only one person at Styles who works on the land, Mrs. Cavendish."

"But the door was locked from the inside!" I cried.

"We only have her word for it. At the inquest she also said she heard the table fall over. You, yourself, Hastings helped me prove that she couldn't have heard it from her room. In fact, I am convinced that Mary Cavendish was in Mrs. Inglebrook's room when the alarm was given."

I glanced at Mary. She was very pale but smiling.

"We will say that she was seeking something and could not find it," Poirot continued. "Suddenly Mrs. Inglebrook wakes and has a fit. She flings out her arm, knocking over the table, and rings the bell. Mary, startled, drops the candle, scattering grease on the carpet. She picks it up and retreats to Cynthia's room, closing the door behind her. This is when her sleeve caught in the bolt. She cannot be seen, but suddenly the servants are arriving. She runs back into Cynthia's room and begins to shake her awake. Nobody saw her arrive, and this is important. Am I right Madame?"

Mary nodded and replied:

"You are quite right. You understand that revealing these facts would not have helped my husband's case."

"Perhaps, but anyway, it clears my mind to pursue other matters."

"The will!" Lawrence cried. "It was Mary who destroyed it!"

She shook her head.

"No," Poirot said. "Only Mrs. Inglebrook could have destroyed the will."

"It's impossible!" I cried.

"Nevertheless, it is true!" Poirot replied. "There can be no other explanation for Mrs. Inglebrook ordering a fire to be lit on the hottest day of the year. You will remember that this household does not waste any paper, because of the war. She had no other way of destroying the will, but I made an error here. I assumed that she had destroyed it, because of her earlier argument, and therefore the argument had taken place *before* the will was destroyed, but there were in fact, two arguments."

The room hushed at this new idea. Poirot continued.

"At four o'clock Mrs. Inglebrook's argument was overheard by Mrs Cavendish. The words she heard were, 'You need not think that any fear of publicity, or scandal between husband and wife will deter me.' I believe they were spoken to John Cavendish. Soon after this, Mrs. Inglebrook made out a new will, calling in the gardeners to sign it, but at five o'clock she used almost the same words when she told Dorcas, 'I don't know what to do; scandal between husband and wife is a dreadful thing.' You will remember Dorcas saw Mrs. Inglebrook holding a piece of paper. She then ordered a fire and burnt it."

Suddenly everyone in the room started whispering. Poirot had to raise his hands to silence us.

"Now," he said. "Something happened between four-thirty and five o'clock to completely change her mind. We know she had no stamps, because she asked Dorcas to bring her some. I believe she tried her husband's desk and found it locked. Desperate, she tried her own keys and found one that fitted. But what did she find inside the desk? A letter from Mr. Inglebrook to Mrs. Raikes. This is what Dorcas saw in her hand. On the other hand, Mrs Cavendish believed it was a letter from her husband to Mrs. Raikes and demanded to see it."

We all looked at Mary Cavendish, but her face revealed no emotion. My eyes were glued to Poirot's for the next part of the story.

"Mrs Cavendish, desperate from jealousy, made a plan to steal the document that night. But chance gave her an advantage here. She found the key to Mr. Inglebrook's desk that had been lost that morning. Sometime in the evening she applied oil to the hinges of the door and then waited until at four o'clock in the morning, when the noise of her movements would seem normal to the maids."

"But Cynthina would have heard her!" I cried.

"Not if there was sleeping powder in Cynthia's coffee from the evening. I checked all six cups and found no sign of this. I was completely stuck until mon ami Hastings told me that Bauerstein was here that evening and had coffee. That made seven cups. And then Lawrence found the missing cup. It tested positive for sleeping powder, as did the cup for Mrs. Inglebrook. Imagine Mrs. Cavendish's horror when Mrs. Inglebrook died! She could only have thought her harmless sleeping powder was to blame! Now we can explain why the strychnine took so long to work. Taken with a sleeping powder its effect is delayed!"

I sighed with pleasure at the simple explanation. Poirot continued.

"But Mrs. Inglebrook never drank the coffee and the cup she used has tested negative for strychnine. So how did the killer give her the dose of poison? The answer is her medicine! The killer needn't have even put it there, because it already contained a small amount of strychnine. This wouldn't have hurt her, but I checked with a chemist and found out that introducing a small amount of bromide creates crystals which drop to the bottom of the bottle. When the last cupful is drunk, it deliverers a lethal dose!"

Poirot's audience gasped. He held up three strips of paper, smiling.

"A letter from the killer."

Poirot read the letter to us all.

Dearest Eve,
You will be worried at hearing nothing. Do not fear! It will be tonight instead of last night. There's a good time coming once the old lady is out of the way. No one can possibly prove the killer was me. That idea of yours about bromides was very clever. But we must be very careful. A single mistake—

"The writer didn't finish!" Poirot said. "But we all know the handwriting."

A howl that was almost a scream broke the silence.

"You devil! How did you get it?" A chair was overturned. Poirot skipped aside. A quick movement by him, and his attacker fell with a crash.

"Messieurs, mesdames," said Poirot, with a sweep of his hand, "let me introduce you to the murderer, Mr. Alfred Inglethorp!"

Marys's London Apartment

Chapter 13—Poirot Explains

A week later Alfred and Eve were in jail, and I was able to speak privately with Poirot.

"Why didn't you tell me it was Alfred!" I asked.

"You might have given the game away without knowing. You are not a man used to hiding his feelings, mon ami, as a detective must be."

"But you gave me no clue!"

"I did! Did I not say that I believed John would be found innocent? And did I not say that I didn't want Alfred arrested *yet*?"

"Ah! Yes. You knew it all along!"

"No. I had much doubt. In fact, I began to think he was innocent."

"What changed your mind?"

"At the inquest, I thought he wanted to be arrested. And then when I discovered that it was not he, but John, that was having an affair with Mr. Raikes, I was sure. You see, that left no reason for Alfred to say nothing about where he was that evening. Unless he truly wanted to be arrested. This had me confused for a while. Then I remembered that your English law does not allow a man to be put on trial twice for the same trial. At the time there was not enough evidence to find Alfred guilty, so he would have been released. That is why he wanted to be arrested!"

"But how did he prove it was not him that went to the chemist's shop?"

"It wasn't him. It was Eve Howard in the disguise! Ingenious, isn't it? It is the perfect crime. The bromides were put in the medicine days before, probably by Eve Howard, knowing she would be far away by the time the last, fatal dose was drunk! The visit to the chemist's was simply to make John look guilty. She even wrote a note inviting John to a remote spot, so that he could not prove he wasn't at the chemist. Instead, I believe he was somewhere in the woods where nobody could have seen him."

"Amazing!"

"Yes. They are both cousins, so while Alfred would have inherited all the money and the house, he would have shared it with Eve. But something went wrong. Mrs. Inglebrook did not take her medicine until a day later, because she had been too busy on the planned day of the murder. Alfred, scared that Eve would panic, wrote her a letter, but Mrs. Inglebrook returned early, so he had to hide it in his desk. She saw him hide it and later used her keys to open the desk."

"She read the note then?"

"Yes. Horrified by the contents of the note she decided to lock it in her own desk. Now she knew danger would come in the form of bromides, but she didn't know from where. As we know, she still hadn't solved this puzzle by the time of her murder. Then the investigation began. Alfred couldn't find his note, but he guessed where it was. He entered her room and forced her desk open with his penknife. Now he had the note, but he couldn't destroy it, because the household did not destroy waste paper. I have also worked out that he only had five minutes to decide what to do. He tore it into strip and hid it in a vase on the mantelpiece. He thought he could return later and take the strips, but knowing some pieces of my own puzzle were missing and that the murderer might return, I had warned the household to watch out for anything suspicious."

"Ah yes! I remember telling you off about this."

"Yes, so Alfred never had the chance to take back the strip of paper."

"I see. But how did *you* find it?"

"I guessed that he might have written such a note, but I couldn't find it! This was the last link, the piece that made me so depressed. And then you gave me the final clue. You reminded me that I had rearranged the vases on the mantelpiece, not once, but twice! Since the room had been locked I thought there could be no reason for somebody to tidy the mantelpiece between these two events, unless something had been hidden in one of the vases!"

"Poirot! You are a genius!"

"Well, the most difficult part was arranging for a woman's happiness. You see, I could have proved John innocent before the trial. But then Mary would not have had to fight so hard for her husband. I don't know if you have seen them since, but now they are the closest couple you could imagine. The trial has brought them so close together that they are very much in love!"

"Well, at least something good has come from it!"

"Not one, but two, things, mon ami. You remember you told me that Lawrence was staring at the far side of the room when Mrs. Inglebrook died?"

"Yes. I wondered about that."

"He saw that Madamoiselle Cynthia's door was unbolted. He immediately thought she was the murderer. That is why he tried so hard to convince us that the death was natural."

"But I don't understand why."

"Lawrence is in love with Cynthia!"

"Oh! She thought he didn't like her!"

"And did she mind?"

"Not at all."

"Then she is in love with *him*."

"Poirot, you know so much about people."

The door opened and Cynthia rushed in. She fidgeted with a little tassel for some moments, then, suddenly exclaimed: "You dears!" She leaned forward, kissed me, then Poirot and rushed out of the room again.

Biography of Lazlo Ferran

Educated near Oxford, during English author Lazlo Ferran's extraordinary life, he has been an aeronautical engineering student, dispatch rider, graphic designer, full-time busker, guitarist and singer, recording two albums. Having grown up in rural Buckinghamshire Lazlo says:

"The beautiful Chiltern Hills offered the ideal playground for a child's mind, in contrast to the ultra-strict education system of Bucks."

After a long and successful career within the science industry, Lazlo Ferran left to concentrate on writing.